COSMOPOLITAN

LOVE **SPELLS**

RITUALS AND INCANTATIONS
FOR GETTING THE
RELATIONSHIP YOU WANT

SHAWN ENGEL

HEARST
books

CONTENTS

MAGICK

CHAPTER 1

THE BASICS OF WITCHCRAFT

CAN I REALLY BECOME A WITCH?

Yes, you can find the power within you to manifest your soulmate and manipulate energy in many different ways, but before we get into that, we have to discuss the art form of magick. To some, the words "witch" or "witch-craft" conjure memories of old Halloween costumes, but an actual Witch is a person who has an intentional practice, understands the vibration of different forms of energy, and can bend said energy to do great things. Rather than flying around on a broomstick, a Witch has dedicated their life to seeing the magick in everything. They identify as a Witch by his or her own choosing, whether they come from a long lineage of witches or newly decide to become one on their own.

However, you don't have to call yourself a Witch to perform, see, or be magick. You are magick, baby.

So what exactly *is* magick? And why the heck is it spelled with a *k*?

Well, magick has a unique meaning for everyone. To me, it's the connection of dreams to reality, elements to creation, and the physical to the metaphysical. Visualization, commitment, and creativity are all essential traits when it comes to performing magick. One must be able to visualize it in order to cast spells, commit to the universe to shape thoughts into reality, and create infinite possibilities for their own destiny. If you can dream it, you can be it—as long as you have the discipline to follow through.

Every magick is an art form.

Spells can be cast in any shape or form you desire, whether you carry out a ritual, embody an energy, or whisper a mantra. The only things that are required of you are desire, commitment to carrying out a spell, and the intuition to know when it needs to be repeated.

Trust me: You will be a boss at spell-casting after you read the first two chapters of this book, but you need to build your foundation in the practice of magick before you can get witchy AF.

INTENTION IS EVERYTHING

In magick, intention is not only important, but mandatory. When practicing spell work and other forms of magick, you must proceed with personal responsibility and with the utmost respect for your environment, and know how you can serve your environment best. So intention—aka, your desire—is the driving force behind your magick. But it comes with a few caveats.

While your intentions must be specific to manifest your desire, you should not expect them to redirect the universe. By calling your wants by name rather than by feeling while practicing magick, you lock out the universe's intention for your destiny.

It's best not to focus on a specific person while casting spells from this book. Your intention should be larger than "Bring my crush to my doorstep." Try instead: "Bring someone to my doorstep that treats me with respect and dignity and lays it down in the bedroom."

There are many practices in witchcraft that stress that your intention should be of the "highest good." While I agree with this in theory, it's important to extract the true meaning of this intention.

For example, if you fall in love, you and your partner are probably going to go out to dinner before you attempt to save the world. This doesn't mean that your love isn't of the highest good! When you fall in love, your energy could impact others in a positive way, which indirectly contributes to society. Besides, we each have a right to happiness, and when it arrives in the form of a great consensual relationship (and the sex is amazing), it is absolutely of the highest good. This is why wishing love on someone who isn't right for you is a waste of energy.

ELEMENTS 101: ENERGY IS EVERYWHERE

Energy describes the currents that move through absolutely everything in life. In case you fell asleep during chemistry class, molecules constantly vibrate, and in terms of witchcraft, the vibrations can occur at different frequencies depending on what elements you're working with. Certain items can contain the frequencies of multiple elements. For now let's stick to the basics, which are the five elements of Witchcraft: Fire, Earth, Air, Water, and Spirit.

Fire carries a spark of passion. It is a creator and a destroyer. When using fire in spells from this book, you can expect a quick return on your intentions—or powerful banishment, if that's what you're after.

Earth energy moves much slower and allows us to stay grounded. Solid matter has molecules that vibrate in place rather than in motion. Use them in spell work by burying an item or using crystals to create a sensation of permanence and anchoring.

Air is fast-paced and energetic, sometimes even more

so than fire. It literally inspires me to speak things into existence with a loud roar. Don't worry, a whisper can pack a powerful punch, too! Intention, not tone, is how you get the job done.

Water is a conduit and is excellent for creation and emotion. Taking a bath, speaking into water, or using water as an offering helps to channel it into realms unseen and connect you psychically to the universe.

Spirit, the last of the five elements in witchcraft, can be a god or a pagan deity, but it should be a higher power that you feel comfortable celebrating. For the sake of this book, we'll refer to spirit as the Universe. Spirit is your connection to what you can't see, and it requires your trust. It has the most impactful vibration and can be felt on your skin when you've truly tapped into magick.

THE MOON

The moon also carries incredible energetic properties. Its cycle, which lasts about 29.5 days, should inform when you work your magick. There are different phases of the moon that are used for different kinds of spells, so take notice of them in order to amplify your spells.

If you want to call something into your life, you should practice your spell work during the New Moon, when the moon has no light and is beginning to wax. Because it's just starting to receive the light of the sun before it continues to "grow," you can expect that any manifestation spell set forth during this phase will be heard and nurtured by the universe. This lasts about two days on each end of the cycle.

If you want to practice repetitive spell work and keep your New Moon manifestation alive, you should cast spells during the Waxing Moon, when light grows on the moon. As long as the light grows, you can expect returns on the intention you set.

Listen up: We'll get into sex magick later (see page 62), but the Full Moon is a prime time to bang it out for a purpose. The Full Moon is the climax of the moon's light and is best utilized for the last push of your intention.

When the moon starts to wane, or lose light, Witches often let go of parts of their intention that did not, or no longer, serve them. Waning Moons are great for the release of any and all things that are not aligned with their highest good.

Finally, the Dark Moon, which is the last phase of the waxing moon before it is new, is perfect for banishment and cord cutting. If you just went through a breakup, the Dark Moon is your friend. Trash all that leftover broken-heartedness during the phase of no light.

ASTROLOGY

Astrology is not necessary to cast spells, be a Witch, or believe in magick. That said, it's a point of interest for most Witches, and it can provide an additional boost of energy into your spells.

Each of the twelve signs of the zodiac are seen as a slice of a pie in the sky, and all of the planets transit into these signs at different times, depending on the planet's speed and size. With Earth as the focus, you can determine where in the sky each of the astrological constellations are. This determines everything from birth charts to the current day's astrology. The moon transits into each sign more frequently because it is small and positioned closest to Earth. You can *reaaaally* study the solar system to make your magick more complex, but for the sake of bringing more energy to your love spells, I suggest that you pay attention to the moon phase and what sign the moon is in.

Tackling the ins and outs of the solar system in this introduction to magick is a bit aggressive, so instead of digging deeper, let's review the twelve signs of the zodiac and the signature energy they bring.

ARIES is an incredibly creative Fire sign that is independent and self-motivated. When casting under this sign, you can expect a quick spark with heavy motivation.

TAURUS is an Earth sign that is very grounded and loves luxury. Taurus energy anchors while it influences beauty.

GEMINI is an Air sign that brings quick wit and communication. The moon in this sign will open up your partner to discussions and make things flirty.

CANCER is the homebody of the Water signs and is perfect for kitchen witchery. Cancer is also very emotional, so it's best to ground yourself when working with this energy.

LEO, a Fire sign, is one of the most fun signs to cast spells under because it has a flair for getting attention. It is my go-to energy for glamour magick.

VIRGO is a very grounded Earth sign, and the sign of service. Utilize this energy when you're reflecting on how you show up in your relationships.

LIBRA is a flirtatious, beautiful, and fun Air sign. While slightly more subdued than Leo, the Lion of the zodiac, Venusian Libra energy is also great for glamour and attraction.

SCORPIO is a sexy Water sign and is the detective of the zodiac. Pair Scorpio energy with sex magick, shadow work, or banishment for powerful results.

SAGITTARIUS is the traveler and philosopher of the zodiac, a Fire sign who isn't tied down easily. When you're looking to line up a few (or a lot) of new boos, I suggest turning to this energy.

CAPRICORN energy is tough, tenacious, and careful. As an Earth sign, this energy provides a big sense of permanence. Capricorn energy can be wonderful for manifesting a very practical love.

AQUARIUS, an Air sign, helps to see the big picture and the good of society. If you're having trouble setting an intention that is of the highest good, you may want to reflect under this energy to gain some clarity.

PISCES, a Water sign, has energy that is deep, sensual, and psychic. Pisces can motivate you to fall head over heels, and it's easy to get lost under this energy. Try not to give in to the seduction. Instead, channel your intuition during this time to see who's really worth hanging around for.

PLACES OF WORSHIP:
HOW TO BUILD AN ALTAR

Witchcraft social media is filled with beautiful spaces decorated with pillar candles, crystals, fancy cups, and statues. Sure, these scenes are Instagrammable, but what do they all mean?

These sacred spaces are altars that are dedicated to deities, energies, concepts, or ancestors. They are spiritual work spaces to bring offerings, a place to ask for guidance and to work with.

Personally, I have many altars. I have one dedicated to money; one to my matron goddess, Freyja; one to love; and one to my grandparents. Each is a space filled with items that exude their energy to me, and I ask them for guidance when needed.

There is no right way to build an altar, except to simply use your intuition! Here are some prompts to help you begin creating your love altar right away:

• Does love have a color?

• Does love have a symbol?

• When you envision love, what does it look like?

• Do any flowers remind you of love?

Any of these answers can be used to influence items on your own unique love altar, and if you visit it often while performing your spells, the Universe will help you to better carry them out!

GODDESSES TO GUIDE YOU

When building an altar, seeking guidance, or merely invoking a sexy energy, there are many goddesses you can work with to help carry out your intentions. Goddess energy provides an extra oomph from the Universe, especially if you aren't feeling certain about the outcome of the spell. It's just one more layer of connection, besides the moon and astrology, that can help you feel in tune with the reality you're trying to manifest. There are many deities from various backgrounds that you can call on during spell work, but I recommend working with these specific goddesses while casting love spells.

VENUS, or Aphrodite in Greek mythology, is the goddess of love, fertility, and prosperity. She is a dynamic goddess to work with. Pictured in Botticelli's painting *The Birth of Venus*, you see the soft lines of a woman emerging from a shell delivered by emotional and creative waters. By calling on her, you are invoking beauty, grace, sexuality, and power.

FREYJA, my matron goddess, is of Norse traditions and governs beauty, magick, and death. She is a complex goddess who not only provokes love and fertility, but also helps the souls of the dead cross over to the other side.

She is a fierce protector who, when called upon, can make you feel like a total badass.

HATHOR, another full-spectrum goddess, comes from Egyptian traditions and is a patron of lovers. She is a goddess of fertility, depicted regularly as a cow. Just as she can incite love, she can destroy humanity. Hathor is wonderful to use in love magick because she creates boundaries and can banish energies that don't serve you.

When working with these goddesses, be respectful and mindful that you are engaging in a relationship with them. Feature them on your altar and know that gifts are welcome!

SPELL-CASTING PROTECTION

The power of psychic protection is an important piece of knowledge to guard yourself with.

There are many ways to protect yourself when performing magick, but the most common method depicted in pop culture is casting a circle. A circle creates a sacred space to practice your magick where you won't be disturbed or influenced by outside forces. Because you are working within a realm unseen, you are able to cast in peace.

You can do an elaborate, *Sabrina*-esque circle, à la

The Craft, or you can just use your finger. Before you cast your circle though, it is also advised that you complete the following steps.

First, be sure to cleanse all your tools and the space in which you are working with smoke. You can use the popularized white sage or palo santo methods (as long as they're ethically sourced), an herb bundle, or incense. Use white sage or palo santo by burning the herb or wood, respectively, and letting the smoke permeate the area. Once the smoke has permeated the area, spin clockwise three times with your finger extended out while asking the elements of witchcraft to protect you. Do not leave this envisioned circle while you cast, because it is now your sacred and protected space. Think of it like an operating room prepped for surgery; it's a sterile environment that will allow you to execute a desired action without the influence of microorganisms, or in the case of magick, spirits!

While in your circle, the next and very crucial step is to ground yourself. Grounding simply means to connect with your body and the Earth to feel metaphysically anchored while you are casting. Each spell calls for a unique way for you to come into your body and connect with the Earth, but the foundation layer should always be grounding.

Once your spell has been carried out, close your circle by thanking the elements while you spin counter-clockwise and envision the circle actually closing. Your visualizations are the most important magickal tool you have, so it's necessary to start stretching that muscle.

If you want to level up your Witch game, you can create your circle using the cardinal directions, adorning each of them with items or candles that represent their respective elements.

For this purpose, you can use these associations:

- **NORTH:** This cardinal direction is represented by Earth. You can use a green candle to represent it, or anything associated with the Earth, like rocks, soil, or plants. You are encouraged to use your imagination in witchcraft.

- **EAST:** This cardinal direction is represented by Air and you can use a yellow candle, or feathers, smoking incense, or whatever your imagination desires.

- **SOUTH:** This cardinal direction is of Fire, and a red candle, cinnamon, peppers, or other fire-related objects should be used.

- **WEST:** This is the cardinal direction of Water, and calls for a blue candle, a dish of water, seashells, or whatever feels like fluid energy.

When creating an ornate circle, be sure to place your items in their corresponding directions. If you are unsure of which way you are facing, use the map app on your phone to point you in the right direction. As you face each item, call on the element it symbolizes while envisioning its presence—for Fire, a crackling flame; for Water, a running stream. Finish by looking up to ask for guidance from your Spirit, who is shining a bright light down on you and the area in which you are casting. To close your circle, thank your elements for their presence in their positions, and envision your energy being balled up and thrust into the sky.

If that seems like too much, just follow the first example and use your finger. Magick should make you feel comfortable, otherwise it won't be effective. Create the circle that feels right to you.

Creating a circle should always be the first step in practicing the spells in this book. Otherwise, you'll be inviting unknown energies into your space that can influence your intention and your home as a whole. Remember to always use protection when you're chasing some sweet, sweet love.

CHAPTER 2

HOW TO MANIFEST LOVE CORRECTLY: THE RULES

MAKE FREE WILL THE THIRD WHEEL IN YOUR RELATIONSHIP

Look, everyone wants to rope someone specific into their lap when it comes to love magick. Time and again I see people who want to cast a spell on an ex they're still in love with, or spark interest in a crush that they've lusted over from afar.

I can tell you, undeniably, that this is a bad move.

Free will is the given right of someone to make their own choices outside of influence. Just as gaslighting, manipulation, isolation, and other acts of abuse in a relationship are not permitted here, neither is creating an energetic environment that robs a human of making their own rational choices.

This book will undoubtedly help you find the love that you desire, but it may not appear the way you pictured it. While your dream bae might seem like the total package, it's best to use the characteristics that make them such a catch when you set an intention rather than calling them directly to your bed. This way the universe is free to wrangle your dream person—or someone better—for the highest good!

The ethics of magick can become a little complicated when a standing relationship is involved.

If you're looking to be more communicative with your partner or crush, the best spell is to start the conversation. The chapter on communication (page 71) will help you to do just that! The emphasis of intention in this scenario is to open up a dialogue about something in particular rather than to chat about all the things.

Further, trying to wrangle someone who ghosted you back into your DMs isn't wise either. When you're trying to hear more from a person who has said everything with their actions, you're asking for more pain.

Passion and desire spells have the same ethics as communication spells. With them, you're creating an opportunity for mind-blowing sex, but you can't expect it to happen in a specific timeframe. Again, if you aren't on the same page sexually with your partner, open communication is the key. Want to hear some real magick? Invoke Venus energy, which will turn your partner into a real beast between the sheets.

Witchcraft is a powerful practice of the self. Thus, it should be fully self-focused. The magickal reality you create should exist in the sphere of everything you have control over. Common decency and consent should never be taken for granted. Think of it as going into a job interview: You can dress the part, slap on a huge smile, and amp up your energies of success, but if you were to force someone to hire you, it would take away their power of choice and could hurt you in the long run.

All things are as they are meant to be.

HOW TO REDIRECT YOUR INTENTIONS

Alright, so now you're stuck.

You bought this book because the hot cashier at the pharmacy doesn't know you exist and you want them to walk you down the aisle tomorrow.

I get it.

Good news: You're not at a total loss. There are many ways to redirect your intentions while spell-casting, meaning that pharma-boo will be ringing you up between the sheets faster than you can pull out your rewards card.

Instead of focusing on a Prince Charming–type scenario where he whisks you away on a white horse that the pharmacy happens to have in storage, visualize yourself striking up a conversation that he receives well.

That way, you've now created an energetic exchange even though the ball is in his court. With glamour magick, like wearing pink lipstick that you've charmed for passion (see page 46), you're inviting in the energy of desire. You've created a scenario with the correct energy for him to make the moves.

In terms of exes, which is a big focus for many who are seeking out love magick, it's very important to stress that things didn't work out because they weren't supposed to. Holding on to a dead relationship is a complete disservice to you and your past boo, and that thought should be banished under a Dark Moon.

You can, however, take what you've learned from your past relationship and use it for bigger magick when you redirect this intention. Making a list of (objective) pros and cons can help you reaffirm what you truly want in a relationship and will help you invoke just that.

Wait until you've healed from your breakup to do this. Fresh wounds on sad bodies make them unfit to cast spells. Give yourself ample grieving time. Then, ground yourself by noticing where your body feels tight and how your feet are rooted into the ground.

Once you feel sturdy, write down everything you admired about your past relationship, and everything that didn't serve you. Use this list to call a love that's better for you, and you'll have far greater success with magick.

BECOME YOUR MOST BADASS SELF

A sign of a healthy relationship is when another person brings out the best in you, and vice versa. So how to best attract your soul mate? Create an environment in which YOU thrive.

If your recipe for a perfect relationship involves both partners being at their best, the first step is for each partner to be at their best. Becoming whole on your own provides the right path for you to invite in or strengthen love.

This is where the beauty of magick, manifestation, and visualization all align. Right now, as you're sitting wherever you are, reading this book, close your eyes for a second and think about you at your absolute best.

What is your attitude like? Your outfit? Your walk? Where are you going?

Think hard about this. Plaster this version of yourself into your mind.

Now, walk the walk.

Just because you may not have six figures in the bank doesn't mean you can't have six-figure energy. Just because you aren't Gigi Hadid doesn't mean you can't have supermodel energy. Just because your clothes aren't Gucci or you don't get a blowout every day doesn't mean that you can't be fabulous AF.

You must embody confidence to call in the greatness that the Universe has to offer you, even if you feel like you're pretending or playing dress-up. This is magick, and the energy shift it creates is absolutely palpable. You'll be amazed at the types of people and opportunities you attract when shifting your mind into your ultimate, most badass self.

If you can't walk around with Beyoncé energy just yet, start dissecting your environment to determine what is making you feel small. You can feel like a prisoner of the routines you've created for yourself, but I'm here to teach you magick, not enable a pity-party. Change your perspective, whether it's in your head or within your routine, and it will help you in miraculous ways.

BREAK DOWN YOUR BARRIERS

So, by now you've probably wondered: "I fantasize about finding true love all the time. If I'm visualizing it, why hasn't it happened yet?"

The answer to this question is simple in context, yet very complicated in extraction.

People often feel, on a deep level or at the surface,

that they ultimately do not deserve the love they desire. And, because the Universe listens to all thought patterns without judgment, it reads these doubts loud and clear.

So, in order to quit this thinking and maximize your chances for success, you must explore what you *think* you deserve in this world. And that takes some brutal honesty on your part.

Throughout our lives, we create stories that become belief systems to support our daily experiences. If we have never had luck in love, it is easier for us to say, "dating is hard," or "men/women/people suck," than to heal from an experience and move on with wisdom, balanced self-respect, and sturdy boundaries.

We turn our story into a self-fulfilling prophecy; if dating is hard, it will *continue* to be hard. If people suck, you'll continue dating people who aren't right for you to support this theory.

So, in order to break this destructive thought pattern, you must analyze it first. What do you believe to be true about love, dating, and the people you lust over? What evidence supports your view of relationships? How do you believe you need to be treated in order to feel loved by someone else?

Challenging negative thoughts will also help you to become more aware, and thus more intentional, in manifestation. If you find yourself obsessively sneering at the way your Tinder date is chewing his food instead of listening to what he's saying, you're unconsciously blinding yourself from what is right in front of you. Instead, if you test your strength by taking the time to find out if your match is the real deal, you'd be doing good detective work in your search for romance.

Bringing these practices to the forefront of your mind will help you to become more open and receptive to love, whether you're in a relationship or not. Understand that negative thoughts and beliefs take dedication and patience to reroute, but it will be beneficial for you in the long run. The Beyoncé version of yourself doesn't cut corners.

These challenges seem terrifying at first, but they become the key to freedom. If you can look at the answers with unashamed curiosity and continue to unpack them with the Self-Love Spells chapter, you will create a blank canvas on which you can paint your fantasy romance.

INSPIRED ACTION

Unfortunately, when you work on specificity, intention, visualization, and consciously breaking down your barriers, Harry Styles doesn't automatically appear naked in your bed.

But that isn't what magick is.

Doing work on yourself should boost your confidence and inspire you to act! When you feel good about yourself, you'll want to book a bae-cation with your partner to spice things up and talk about your true feelings. If you're single, you'll want to strap on your slinkiest LBD and collect numbers during a girls' night out.

When you're feeling on top of the world, you won't put up with the BS that has tainted your belief system for so long.

So, the key here is to pump yourself up and act when you feel inspired. Who knows, maybe the cashier at the pharmacy will give you their number now that you're feeling confident enough to call.

Use that energy to guide you into taking some risks because, ultimately, that's where the magick is made.

CHAPTER 3

SELF-LOVE SPELLS

As RuPaul says, "If you can't love yourself, how the hell you gonna love someone else?"

It's an adage that will always be true: If you can't look in the mirror and shower yourself with affection when it counts, how can you invite that energy in from the outside? By working to love yourself unconditionally, you can create a blueprint for how you'll receive love in return.

REFLECTION SPELL

Although this spell is simple to perform, it is highly powerful. Use it as often as you need until you feel like the badass that you are. Within this practice, you will be forcing an affirmation deep into your subconscious that will allow you to glow from the inside out.

YOU WILL NEED

A mirror • Your honesty

TIMING

This spell is best performed under New Moon energy. Any astrological placement fits well with this type of affirmation spell, but fiery Aries energy will light it up.

METHOD

- Cast your circle around you and your mirror. Start to ground yourself. Notice how heavily your feet feel rooted into the ground, and work your way up your body, noticing any areas of tightness. When you feel secure, look directly into the mirror to begin the spell.

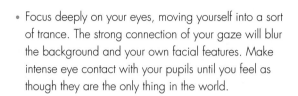

- Focus deeply on your eyes, moving yourself into a sort of trance. The strong connection of your gaze will blur the background and your own facial features. Make intense eye contact with your pupils until you feel as though they are the only thing in the world.

- As you fixate into the depths of your pupils, repeat, "I am powerful, desirable, good, and whole. I am worthy of love that nurtures and supports me. I am all that I need, and what I want flows effortlessly to me." Repeat this three times, then clap your hands to shake yourself out of the trance. Close your circle and carry this energy throughout your day.

ROSE QUARTZ MEDITATION

Think of meditation as a mental vacation where you can escape from a barrage of harmful thoughts that you have created for yourself. Using this practice will help overcome these thoughts and make you love yourself for who you are. This spell will take some practice if meditation is new to you, but the more you perform it, the better you will feel.

YOU WILL NEED

A piece of rose quartz, any size • A quiet place to sit

TIMING

This spell is best performed every morning throughout the course of a Full Moon cycle. This way, you'll be learning to love yourself with different influences of various astrological placements.

METHOD

- Ground yourself by inhaling for three counts, holding your breath for three counts, exhaling for three counts, and holding your breath out for three counts. Continue this pattern until you feel calm. Sink deeply into the ground.

- Take your rose quartz in your dominant hand and hold it at your heart. Concentrate on the stone's vibrations, held near your energy center.

- As you feel grounded and still, envision the rose quartz connecting with your heart by linking a bright pink light with your chest. Envision this pink light growing down through your stomach, over your legs, and down through your feet. Now envision this light growing up your neck and covering your head until its circumference surrounds your entire body and invigorates you like a huge, energetic hug.

- Sit here until you feel comfortable, then close your circle and carry yourself with this pink light at your heart's center throughout the day.

PINK CANDLE CARVING

This spell calls for fire and creativity. Dedicate a solid amount of time to carrying it out. Using a flame and intentional invention, you create an imprint in the Universe for the person you want to be, exactly as you see it. It's best to only perform this manifesting spell once per moon cycle because, while candle magick works quickly, it's powerful and should not be repeated too often, especially when burning seven-day candles.

YOU WILL NEED

A pink candle, any size, but preferably a pillar candle • A wooden pick • Olive oil • Pink glitter (optional)

TIMING

This spell is best performed under a Full Moon. The best astrological moons to work with are the any of the Fire signs (Aries, Leo, or Sagittarius). I personally prefer Leo.

METHOD

• Get centered and begin to envision your best self. Sit with this ideal person until you feel the vibrations of him or her coursing through you. Then, with this enlightened vision of yourself held in your mind's eye, use your wooden stick to carve your name into the pink candle.

- Olive oil is ruled by the sun and is great for healing. Coat your hands in it, then, beginning at each end of your candle, cover the entire shaft. This is called dressing your candle.

- Sprinkle the pink glitter where you carved your name. This reflects your vision of yourself into the energy of the flame.

- Light your candle and stare into the flame, burning your vision of your best self into the fire.

- Close your circle, and let your candle burn all the way down to complete the manifestation. If you must put out the candle, don't blow it out. Snuff it out so it retains the intention.

DIVINATION SPREAD

A deck of tarot cards be helpful in self-discovery. Personally, it has helped me understand the spectrum of characteristics that people and environments can inhabit, and it has allowed me to see that lessons can be labeled outside of the paradigm of "bad" and "good."

The tarot asks for gratitude, which is very enlightening.

YOU WILL NEED

Tarot or oracle cards

TIMING

This spell is best performed under a Waning Moon so you can let go of what doesn't serve you. All Water signs nurture this kind of emotional healing, but a moon in Scorpio is optimal.

METHOD

- Ground yourself by becoming aware of your breath and feeling where your body is tense.

- Shuffle the cards until you feel confident, then pull three cards in a way that makes sense to you. Some readers pick from the top, some the middle, and some the bottom. The cards will tell you how to pull.

How I view myself	What I struggle with	How to heal

- Read your cards based on the guide that comes with your deck and explains their meanings, and reflect on how they relate to you. The placement of the cards will tell you how they relate to your life in that very moment.

- Close your circle and continue to think about the messages of this spread throughout your day.

- Reading tarot can be challenging, so be sure to use your intuition to extract the cards' significance. If the answers aren't obvious, try journaling about your experience and see how the messages of the cards show up in your life.

- If you aren't familiar with this type of divination, you may want to employ a professional to read your cards for you.

BATH POTION

Bath magick is very spiritous because you are immersing yourself in water, an element that carries energy and makes things happen. This spell requires a bathtub, but if you only have a shower, you can create this potion in a bowl and pour it over you while cleansing. Be sure to coat your entire body with the potion.

YOU WILL NEED

Lemons • Rose petals • Rose quartz • Lavender essential oil

TIMING

This spell is best performed in the evening under New Moon energy. The best astrological signs to work with are Taurus and Libra because both signs are ruled by Venus, the goddess of love.

METHOD

- Draw a bath of warm water. Slice the lemons into fours, and place the slices in the water. Lemons are ruled by the sun and are linked to the solar plexus, your belly chakra. Engaging the two will increase your confidence.

- Sprinkle rose petals into the bath. This will increase the energy for luxury, beauty, and Venusian properties, such as money and attraction.

- Place your rose quartz in the bath so it charges the water with the self-love energy it carries.

- Finally, place a few drops of lavender essential oil in the bath to invite calmness and relaxation.

- Get into the bath and ground yourself by scanning your body, noticing any areas of tightness. Breathe deeply.

- Envision a bright yellow light emerging from your stomach and a bright green light growing from your heart. Connect the yellow light to your solar plexus chakra and the green light to your heart chakra. This will help you love with more confidence.

- Place the rose petals on your body and feel their beauty sinking deep into your skin. As you bathe in this energy, feel yourself connecting to your body and the light that it holds.

- When you are ready, end the bath by releasing the water down the drain. As it funnels away, envision all your self-doubt rushing away with it.

- Close your circle and carry this energy with you to bed.

SHADOW WORK

This may sound counterintuitive, but shadow work is actually the practice of casting light on the traits that you like least about yourself so you can nurture them with kindness and understanding. When we thrust our bad habits into the shadows, we selectively become blind to them, which stops us from receiving our desires. Although shadow work is challenging, the payoff is very rewarding. For all spells, but this one in particular, be sure to ground yourself.

YOU WILL NEED

A pen • Paper • Your honesty

TIMING

This spell is best performed under Waning Moon energy. Scorpio energy is great for exploring the shadows, but Pisces energy opens your intuitive emotions. Earth-sign energy (Taurus, Virgo, and Capricorn) can help first-time shadow workers get grounded before they begin their emotional exploration.

METHOD

- Stand and root your feet into the ground. Work your way up your body, addressing any tightness that is present. When you feel secure, journal on the following prompts:

  ✦ When do I feel loved?

  ✦ When do I feel rejected?

  ✦ What do I know about receiving affection? Is it the same as love and respect?

- How do I speak to myself when I'm disappointed or anxious? Does my speech align with what love means to me?

- Meditate on your answers and try not to judge yourself.

- Close your circle and carry this newfound awareness into your day-to-day relationships.

GODDESS INVOCATION

Use the list of goddesses (pages 15–16) for this spell or pick another goddess that resonates with you by focusing on the divine energy that you'd like to portray. For example, if you're interested in a Venus invocation, see page 118.

YOU WILL NEED

Sexy lingerie • A mirror

TIMING

This spell is best performed under a New Moon. Fire signs (Aries, Leo, Sagittarius) and Venusian signs like Libra or Taurus work well.

METHOD

- Get naked (if you dare!) and, as directed on page 118, cleanse your aura and the lingerie with smoke.

- Stand tall, like a large, flowing tree, and root your feet into the ground. Work your way up your body, addressing any tightness that is present. Breathe in deeply and vigorously exhale from the belly.

- As you put on your lingerie, envision your goddess of choice pouring into you from the top of your head, filling your body with sexy, sensual energy.

- Look at yourself in the mirror in your lingerie and see yourself as a goddess. Breathe in power, beauty, and grace, and breathe out self-doubt, harmful thoughts, and any trace of nervousness. Breathe deeply for as long as you need.

- Close your circle and wear your lingerie under your clothes for the day, envisioning yourself walking around as a goddess on Earth.

LIPSTICK CHARM

This is a fun kind of glamour magick to perform daily. Your lipstick or lip gloss is front and center on your face, and it commands attention and respect. Throughout your day, notice how you receive energy and modify your visualizations accordingly for the maximum effect.

YOU WILL NEED

Your favorite pink lipstick • Mirror

TIMING

This spell is best performed under New Moon energy. Venusian signs like Libra and Taurus work well, and other Air signs like Aquarius and Gemini spark communication. Leo's flirtatious energy is also great for this charm.

METHOD

- Standing in front of your mirror, ground yourself by breathing in and out deeply. Focus on your lipstick and envision yourself as a flirty, sensual, successful goddess.

- As you swipe the lipstick onto your lips, hold that vision in your mind's eye.

- Repeat the phrase, "I am as desirable as I believe I am," three times.

- Blow yourself a kiss in the mirror to complete the charm.

- Close your circle and carry yourself with this energy throughout your day.

SELF-LOVE TAPPING RITUAL

This healing ritual can be used in many different scenarios, such as quitting a bad habit, focusing on deeper breaths, or manifesting prosperity. For this practice, we will focus on self-love, but you are encouraged to change the affirmation based on where you want to strengthen your relationships.

YOU WILL NEED

Yourself!

TIMING

This spell is best performed daily, starting on a New Moon. Any Earth placements (Taurus, Virgo, Capricorn) will help ground you while Air placements (Gemini, Libra, Aquarius) will you communicate.

METHOD

- Ground yourself while sitting. Notice how heavily your body feels rooted into the ground, then scan yourself from head to toe to identify any areas of tightness.

- When you feel settled, tap along your pinky finger with the opposite hand, as listed in the diagram below.

- As you tap the karate-chop point, repeat this phrase three times: "Even though I don't always feel my most confident, beautiful, or powerful, I deeply and completely love and accept myself." Then move on to the pattern in the diagram.

- Once you have tapped into the karate-chop source, start moving around the points that are listed in the diagram while repeating that affirmation. Continue doing rounds of this tapping (from karate-chop to underarm) until you feel a shift.

- Close your circle and carry yourself with this energy throughout your day.

TAPPING POINTS

1. Karate chop (outside hand)
2. Top of head
3. Inner eyebrow
4. Under eye
5. Under nose
6. Chin
7. Breast bone
8. Under arm

CHAPTER 4

ATTRACTION SPELLS

Attraction is one of the most sought-after energies. Who doesn't want to have all eyes on them when they enter a room?

The practice of receiving attention deals with exerting the right energy and knowing exactly what you want. These spells will have you feeling sexier and more sure of yourself than ever. That confidence is going to radiate outward, drawing in the objects of your desire.

When you feel your best, people are automatically attracted to you because they want to feel just as self-assured as you do! Confidence is the sexiest trait and will have your suitors beating down your metaphysical door. If you need extra help finding your mojo and embodying your inner goddess, return to the previous chapter to amp up your sensual energy.

GLAMOUR MAGICK

This spell takes the lipstick charm to a whole new level. Use the intention of glamour to increase your attraction skills on a day when you want to meet someone new.

YOU WILL NEED

Your fiercest outfit • Makeup • A mirror

TIMING

This spell is best performed under New Moon to Full Moon energy so you can bring in a new flame. Fire signs spark this blaze while Air signs will increase communication for flirting.

METHOD

- Ground yourself by breathing in confidence and exhaling self-doubt. Once you feel centered, grab your glamour tools.

- Select an outfit that makes you feel absolutely gorgeous. Insecurities cannot stand in your way when your intention is to attract a mate. Whatever makes you feel most attractive will make you appear the most attractive.

- Once you are dressed, use the mirror to apply makeup that makes you feel comfortable. If you don't normally contour your face like Kim Kardashian, don't try to do so for this spell. We're trying to amp up your natural energy, not make you feel like you're wearing a costume.

- Once you are ready for the day, stare into the mirror and repeat, "I am fierce and I am strong, and the right person will come along," three times.

- Close your circle and carry this energy throughout your day.

RED CANDLE CARVING

You can expect an eruption of passion from this spell. Be sure to keep your options open in visualizing, and instead of focusing on the person you want to attract, envision how you want him or her to make you feel. This spell will help attract the perfect match into your life, if only for one night in the bedroom.

YOU WILL NEED

A red candle (preferably a pillar candle) •
A dowel • Olive oil • Cinnamon

TIMING

This spell is best performed from a New Moon to a Full Moon. Stick with Fire signs for this kind of candle magick, or Scorpio for an added layer of sexy.

METHOD

- Ground yourself by noticing any tightness in the body and sink deep into relaxation.

- Begin dressing your candle. Using the dowel, carve a heart into the top of the candle.

- Continue by bringing olive oil in from the ends, and then sprinkle it with cinnamon to increase heat and passion. During the dressing process, envision passionate sex with a person who has everything you desire.

- Light your candle and let it burn all the way down, noticing any changes in the flame. If you cannot leave your candle burning unattended, snuff it out so you don't blow out the intention along with the flame.

- Close your circle and keep your candle burning in a safe place.

VISION BOARD MANIFESTATION

This spell will help you define your desires and put them in front of your mind's eye. By visualizing the physical representation of what you want, you are more clearly able to call it into reality. Use this vision board to manifest a long-term relationship between you and your S.O.

YOU WILL NEED

Magazines, especially previous issues of
Cosmo! • Poster board

TIMING

This spell is best performed under New Moon energy to set the intention. Earth signs are best for creating this foundation.

METHOD

- Center yourself and begin to envision a successful relationship and all of the details that make it ideal.

- Flip through your magazines and find representations of this perfect union, whether it's traveling with your bae, staying at home and cooking a meal, or glamorous nights out with your friend. Cut them out one by one, with intention.

- Glue, tape, or pin your cutouts to your poster board, and hang your collage where you will regularly see it.

- Close your circle, and trust that it will happen for you.

PAST TENSE LETTER

This is a simple yet powerful manifestation spell. Be very clear about what you want and deserve because the universe will listen.

YOU WILL NEED

A pen and paper

TIMING

This spell is best performed under a New Moon to set the seed for manifestation. Water signs will help you tap into your innermost desires and psychically project them.

METHOD

- Ground yourself by noticing your breath and feeling where your body is tense. Then sink deep into the ground beneath you.

- Begin to write a letter in the past tense to the person you wish to be in a relationship with.

- Start by saying something like, "Thank you so much for being the most supportive, loving, passionate husband I could ever dream of." Don't be afraid to fantasize and get as specific as possible!

- After writing your letter, fold the paper three times. Keep it in your bedside drawer or under your mattress.

- Close your circle and remember to trust the Universe.

FIRE RITUAL

This is a fun ceremony that will make you feel especially witchy. If you have a cauldron on hand, use it, baby! If not, use a stockpot that you have in your kitchen to burn this concoction safely. Be sure to cleanse it with smoke, and proceed with caution.

YOU WILL NEED

A cauldron or a stockpot •
Rose petals • Cinnamon • Bay leaf •
A pen • A lighter • White vinegar

TIMING

This spell is best performed under New Moon energy. Use Fire signs to help amplify a quick return on your cauldron spell.

METHOD

- Toss the rose petals into your cauldron one by one, envisioning how it feels to be cared for and swept off your feet.

- Sprinkle your cinnamon over the petals, envisioning a hot, passionate romance.

- Finally, using your pen, write what you'd like to manifest on your bay leaf. Examples include love, romance, or an unforgettable hookup.

- Carefully light the bay leaf on fire and toss it into your cauldron, letting the flames burn your ingredients in a controlled environment. When the fire goes out on its own, the spell is done.

- Close your circle and wash your cauldron or pot with white vinegar.

SEX MAGICK MANIFESTATION

Sex magick, the act of using orgasms to focus energy into the Universe, is extremely powerful and requires practice, but it's the most fun you'll ever have practicing! All witchcraft requires you to concentrate your energy toward a desire, and using that desire to help you focus will work like a charm.

YOU WILL NEED

A safe and private place to practice • Any toys or tools you desire for solo play

TIMING

This spell is best performed under Full Moon energy, as this is the climax of the moon cycle. Scorpio energy is perfect for sex magick, but Fire signs work just as well for heating things up.

METHOD

• Ground yourself by breathing deeply in and out. Start to set the mood with whatever turns you on, like lighting candles, using essential oils, playing music, or anything else.

- Get into a comfortable position on your bed and begin to touch yourself with your fingers or use your favorite toys. Take time to enjoy how it feels.

- Lose yourself in the motions. Wait until you begin to feel an O coming on.

- Once you're close, focus very clearly in your mind's eye on the relationship you want to attract.

- As you climax, all of the energy that you have released will be targeted at that particular desire and will return to you.

- Close your circle once you feel relaxed, and trust that the Universe has heard you loud and clear (perhaps in more ways than one).

SIGIL CREATION

For this spell, you'll be creating a sigil or magickally charged symbol that will transplant your desire wherever you place it! The energetic properties within sigils hold your intention.

YOU WILL NEED

A pen • Paper

TIMING

This spell is best originated under New Moon energy, when a new cycle begins. Earth energy is really valuable for the material properties of this spell, so use it in conjunction with Virgo, Capricorn, and especially Venusian Taurus.

METHOD

- Ground yourself by taking deep, intentional breaths, and begin to write a list of all of the qualities you desire in a partner. Jot down as many as you'd like. (Yes, "tall" can be one of them.)

- Once you have your list of adjectives, begin to cross out all the vowels in these words. Next, cross out all repeating consonants.

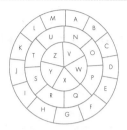

- Once you have one of every consonant and no vowels in sight, take the wheel pictured above and begin to trace the letters out into a symbol.

  For example, if you wrote the words "sweet, caring, affectionate," you would be left with S W T C R N G F, and your sigil would look like this:

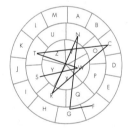

  Once you have the draft of your sigil, rub your hands quickly back and forth together, creating heat and friction. Charge your sigil by putting the heat from your hands over it while you envision the things you desire.

- Close your circle and draw this sigil anywhere you like.

ROSE WATER RECIPE

Rose water is a very easy tincture to make and carries the romantic essence of this Venusian flower. Plus, it smells REALLY good. This spell makes for a great everyday perfume, a face toner, or even a cleaning solution for your floors. The shelf life on natural rose water is not long, so watch for any mildew that may appear in a week's time. Until then, anoint your neck with this mixture to attract a lover, use it as a facial spritz during your at-home pampering, or use it when washing your floors to call in a domestic love.

YOU WILL NEED

About 1 cup of rose petals • About 1½ cups distilled water • A stockpot • A spray bottle

TIMING

This spell is best performed under New Moon energy to align with the beginning of your intention. Venusian signs like Libra and Taurus work extremely well with roses. So do Cancers, in terms of partners you can bring home to Mom.

METHOD

- Ground yourself by breathing deeply, beginning a body scan that starts from the top of your head and ends at your toes. Notice any tension.

- Place your pot on the stove over high heat. Begin to fill your pot with the rose petals while you set an intention for beauty and attraction.

- Pour the distilled water into the pot, barely covering the petals. Playing romantic music or singing some Adele (well, her happy music) will increase the flow of energy.

- Let the water come to a boil, then turn down the heat and let the rose petals simmer until they are colorless.

- Let your mixture cool. Once cool, strain the rose water into a spray bottle.

- Close your circle and keep your rose water in a cool and dry place when it's not in use.

HEART CHAKRA OPENING

There are seven energetic spheres within us that exist as the chakra system. When our bodies are out of alignment, it is said that one or more of these spheres is either too open or too closed. When we struggle with attracting our soulmate, the trouble might be that our heart's center is closed off. If you use this meditation in tandem with tapping (see page 48) or shadow work (see page 42), you can begin to open yourself up to love by understanding your emotional blocks.

YOU WILL NEED

Your visualization

TIMING

This spell is best performed consistently, starting on the New Moon all the way to the Full Moon. Any Water signs will help connect you to your emotions. Leo is a great sign to meditate under since it rules the heart.

METHOD

- Ground yourself by imagining roots growing from your feet deep into the ground, twisting into the Earth's center and anchoring you.

- Get into a comfortable seated position and begin to envision a soft green light radiating from your heart's center.

- Cast your feelings into this light and, as you focus, make it grow brighter and bigger until it is completely illuminating your body.

- Once you begin to feel a shift, you'll know you have started to open up your heart chakra.

- Close your circle and carry yourself with this energy throughout your day.

CHAPTER 5

COMMUNICATION SPELLS

The best relationships require open and honest communication, and the number one way to cultivate that is to get it going yourself! Whether you're flirting, expressing your feelings, or getting to the root of the problem, it takes courage to use your voice.

Wanna know a secret? Your voice deserves to be heard, too.

We tend to hold back our thoughts, feelings, and emotions in fear of rejection or of getting blowback from others. After a while, they can bubble to the surface in catastrophic ways, or they never make it to the surface and we don't get what we want. Assuming that our partners are mind readers often causes confusion and hurt feelings, so assert yourself to open up healthy communication.

Use this chapter to gain confidence to start some real talk, but also use it to flirt! Dialog does not always need to be confrontational or scary—it can be fun!

LAPIS LAZULI CHARM

This spell uses the power of crystals to energize your throat chakra to help you find the courage to speak up in any scenario. Crystals have ancient vibrations because they were formed in the Earth over time (up to millions of years). So yeah, they can powerfully influence us with their magick. Use this charm regularly if you need help with clear communication.

YOU WILL NEED

Lapis lazuli or any other blue stone such as amazonite, blue apatite, or chrysocolla

TIMING

This spell is best performed under New Moon to Full Moon energy so you can bring in healthy communication. Air signs are perfect for this charm because they are the guides of communication. Virgo, which is ruled by Mercury (the planet of communication), will also suffice.

METHOD

- Ground yourself by breathing in confident energy and exhaling self-doubt. Once you feel centered, grab your crystal.

- Lapis lazuli is tied to your throat chakra, but any other blue stone will have a communicative property as well.

- While in a comfortable position within your circle, settle into a meditation while holding your chosen stone. Envision yourself speaking freely and clearly. Imagine what it would be like if you showed up and spoke honestly, with integrity. Visualize this thought directly into your stone until you feel energy pulsing from it.

- Whisper to your stone, "Help me speak my truth," and snap yourself out of the meditative state.

- Close your circle and carry this stone throughout your day.

TIP Bonus points if you complete this spell with a blue stone on a necklace or chain. After enchanting the crystal, wear it around your neck to amplify your voice.

SUN SPELL

The sun is an extremely influential source of energy that is necessary for things to grow and thrive. Because the sun is masculine in nature, which is traditionally associated with taking action, this spell will help you open up and bloom with its warm energy.

YOU WILL NEED

A jar • Filtered water • A pen • Paper •
A sunny window

TIMING

This spell is best performed on a New Moon to invoke a new intention. Leo is the best energy to perform this spell since it is ruled by the sun, but any Air sign will help carry out your communication.

METHOD

- Ground yourself by breathing deeply in and out, relaxing into your practice.

- Fill your jar with the filtered water and hold the jar in your hands, envisioning a confident and flirtatious new you.

- Take your pen and write your name on a corner of the paper. Rip it off gently and place it in the jar.

- Whisper into the jar, "Sunshine and warmth, help me grow."

- Close your circle and keep your jar in a sunny window so the rays of the sun can assist you in opening up and speaking with all the confidence in the world.

THROAT CHAKRA OPENING

When we are unable to express ourselves or feel afraid to use our voice, our throat chakra is probably closed. If it is too open, we may experience "word vomit." This spell will help to open up your throat chakra and bring it into alignment so that you can speak freely.

YOU WILL NEED

Visualization

TIMING

This meditation can be done under any phase of the moon cycle, but New Moons are always best for intention-setting. Air signs are best for opening up this chakra.

METHOD

- Ground yourself by focusing on how the breath feels as it passes through your esophagus. Envision a blue light emanating from your throat, glowing brightly.

- Fixate on the blue light and let it grow so large that it envelops your entire body.

- Start to feel a charge of energy from the blue light's growth. Visualize yourself harnessing the energy and light to your throat. Begin to hum to create an energetic vibration.

- Sit in this trance for as long as it feels comfortable, then, clap to come out of it.

- Close your circle and carry this energy with you throughout the day.

OPEN DOOR SPELL

Speaking our truth can be difficult when we don't know what our truth is. This spell will help you open doors of metaphysical communication by bringing in signs and guides that will point you in the right direction. If you've been waiting to have a tough conversation, this spell will invoke your ability to have it out by allowing you to communicate your grievances effectively.

YOU WILL NEED

Eucalyptus oil • Your front door

TIMING

This spell is best performed under a Waning Moon to release what is standing in your way. Water signs will help you to tap deep into your emotions, but if you are prone to drowning in your feels, you may want to reach for Earth signs to ground you.

METHOD

- Ground yourself by noticing any tightness in the body, doing a full-body scan starting from the top of your head, down to your toes.

- Anoint your front door with the oil, placing a dab in all four corners while you envision the best version of your conversation.

- Eucalyptus oil heals the past and brings a fresh perspective to new situations, so be sure you inhale deeply when you're anointing yourself.

- Close your circle and inspire courage to bring up your feelings!

TALKATIVE TEA RECIPE

Each of the herbs used in this recipe have different energetic properties that help with communication and focus so you can listen as well as you speak. Lavender soothes, star anise improves memory and reception, and cinnamon creates a warm environment in which a conversation can thrive. Too much cinnamon might add too much heat, so be cautious of your proportions. Drink this tea on your own or serve it to your crush/partner to help them open up.

YOU WILL NEED

A teapot • A pinch of lavender •
1 cinnamon stick • 2 star anise • A cup
• Honey (optional) • A teaspoon, for stirring

TIMING

Choose your phase of the moon by the intention you set for this spell. If you're looking to clear the air, aim for Waning. If you're looking to stimulate a conversation with a new crush, go for New and Waxing. Air signs are always best for communication, but Water signs assist in accessing emotion and compassion.

METHOD

- Ground yourself by envisioning roots growing from the soles of your feet deep into the Earth that anchor you like a tall tree.

- Boil the water in your teapot, and begin to envision an open conversation.

- Steep your ingredients for as long as you want.

- As you pour your tea into your cup, keep your vision strong in your third eye.

- You may use some honey to sweeten the conversation if you desire.

- Using the teaspoon, stir your tea in a clockwise direction three times while whispering into the cup, "Let us speak freely, let us listen. And the result will bring more bliss in."

- Close your circle and enjoy your tea.

TECH WITCH PHONE CHARM

It's 2019, and it's about time that spells incorporated technology. This spell literally helps you "call in" your crush! The thing is, it only works if you have their number, so you might want to revisit previous spells to get up the courage to ask for it if you haven't yet.

YOU WILL NEED

Your phone

TIMING

This spell is best performed under New Moon and Waxing Moon energy since you're looking to spark communication. Air signs are going to be great for this spell, but Mercury ruling Virgo will also work.

METHOD

- Ground yourself by breathing deeply in and out, focusing on your throat and heart chakras. Begin to envision your phone ringing or texts/DMs coming in from your crush.

- Once you have a strong visualization and you start to feel the excitement building from receiving their call, go into your contacts.

- Change your crush's name to "I want to talk to you," and while you do that, hold the energetic vibration of your excitement.

- Close your circle and get ready to communicate!

TIP These spells tend to work immediately, so if you don't hear anything in a week, this person is on another energetic level and it's time to move on.

EVOKING COMMUNICATION
WITH COLOR

Color has different energetic frequencies depending on the tone and hue. This is why some spells require specific candle and crystal colors. Wearing a particular color can also evoke a conversation when worn with intention. You can even use color magick with your lipstick!

YOU WILL NEED

A blue outfit

TIMING

This spell is best performed under New Moon energy to start bringing in intention. As always, Air signs will ignite communication but Venusian signs like Libra and Taurus work extremely well with fashion and glamour spells like this one. Life-of-the-party Leo will always inspire when it comes to sparking conversation.

METHOD

- Ground yourself by visualizing an open stream of communication directed at someone in particular, or just in general. Visualize to your specific taste, and then start building your outfit.

- It's good to begin with a blue dress, blouse, shirt, or jacket because they sit close to your throat and heart. This will help people to see you with compassion and courage.

- A very true blue will access deep emotion in terms of communication. A hue mixed with green will open the heart chakra while one mixed with purple will help to access intuition. A lighter shade of blue, mixed with white, will keep things fun and flirtatious. Choose how to construct your outfit based on these hues.

- Accessorizing intentionally will help as well. The energy of blue earrings will show the world that you are a good listener, and a blue necklace will help you to use your voice.

- Once you've chosen your outfit, charge it by envisioning your intention while you get dressed.

- Close your circle and carry your intention throughout the day.

BLUE CANDLE CARVING

If you've been feeling like something isn't right in your relationship but you can't quite put your finger on it, it might be time for some soul-searching. This spell will help start a tough conversation and deliver divine messages for guidance. Repeat this spell once per moon cycle and use with a clear mind so you can be adequately receptive to divine messages. This is best to perform when you have a good amount of time to dedicate to it.

YOU WILL NEED

A blue candle, any size, but preferably a pillar candle • Eucalyptus oil • Oregano

TIMING

This spell is best performed under Full Moon energy to receive guidance. Air signs will always allow for the best communication, but all other signs work as well. Water will help open you up to psychic messages. Earth will keep you grounded if you're feeling super emotional, while Fire is generally great for candle spells (duh).

METHOD

- Center yourself by grounding, doing a body scan from the top of your head to your toes, and sink to the ground before taking your items into your hands.

- With an open third eye and a clear mind, breathe deeply and allow clarity to break through negative thought patterns or any other mud that enters your brain.

- Take your eucalyptus oil, which is great for opening up; coat your hands with it; and cover your candle in from the two ends to dress it.

- Sprinkle the oregano, a Mercury-ruled herb, onto the candle. Try to keep yourself open and clear as you do so.

- Light your candle and stare into the flame, keeping your mind blank and ready to receive.

- Close your circle and let your candle burn all the way down to complete the spell. If you must put out the candle, snuff it out, don't blow it out, to retain the intention. While the candle burns, be aware of any messages you may receive.

CHAPTER 6

SWEETENING SPELLS

I f you're interested in creating a sweet and affectionate vibe for you and your boo, this is the chapter for you!

Many practices within witchcraft are quite logical and literal. If you're looking to sweeten things up or receive some pleasant attention, just add sugar.

If you're in the middle of a cold front with your partner, these spells will warm things up in no time. But be mindful: as with any other section, if these spells do not work after continued effort, it might be time to move on. This section is meant to create an environment in which you and your partner can live like two happy clams, but if they are unwilling to change, the root of the problem is deeper than magick can fix.

On the flipside, if bae needs help opening up, all of these spells will do the trick. Happy casting (and prepare your sweet tooth)!

HONEY JAR SPELL

Jar spells work by creating a closed environment in which you can create your perfect metaphorical reality. Witches have been using jar spells for centuries, and the magick is always apparent. This spell uses honey to sweeten your relationship, so if you've hit a rough patch, use this in conjunction with open communication spells (pages 71–87) and prepare for a shower of affection. However, if your partner is resistant to being sweet, this spell may backfire. Use it with caution and be honest with yourself about the state of your relationship.

YOU WILL NEED

A pen • Paper • Jar • Raw organic honey

TIMING

This spell is best performed under New Moon to Full Moon energy so you can bring in sweetness. Venusian signs such as Libra or Taurus present good timing for this spell because of their romantic qualities. Water signs also help to access deep emotion that will open the doors for affection.

METHOD

- Ground yourself by breathing in optimism and exhaling pessimism. Once you feel centered, take your pen and paper in your hands.

- Write your name and your partner's name on the slip of paper. If you are single and have your eye on someone, you can use this spell for attraction by writing your crush's name.

- As you write, envision yourself in bliss with the eye of your desire and focus that energy into the slip of paper.

- Take your honey and dab it on the paper, coating it until your intuition tells you to stop.

- Place your honey-coated paper in a jar and seal it tight.

- Close your circle and place your jar in a safe spot, like your altar. It now contains your energy and will help to mimic it in reality.

BE-SWEET-TO-GET-SWEET
MEDITATION

Have you noticed that when you complain, your perception starts to throw off your energy, which makes you feel like trash? Well, when you practice magick, you become a mirror for yourself. This spell will exert the energy you wish to see by neutralizing complaints. It can be used in any social situation and is best performed in the morning and carried intentionally throughout the day.

YOU WILL NEED

A strong visualization

TIMING

This spell is equally powerful during all phases of the moon. New Moon Waxing to Full will help you evoke a sweet environment, and Full Waning to Dark will help release negativity. Libra, both an air and Venusian sign, is the best energy to perform under because it is the sweetest sign in the zodiac!

METHOD

- Ground yourself by closing your eyes and breathing deeply in and out, relaxing deeply into your practice. Complete a full-body scan starting from the top of your head down to the tips of your toes and focus on breathing in positivity and breathing out more positivity.

- As you are breathing, in your mind's eye, focus on putting out that sweet energy you desire.

- Picture yourself inhaling and exhaling a cotton candy–pink light. Burn that visualization in your mind and hold it there. Neutralize any negative thought pattern that passes through you with the pink light. Imagine the light zapping it away.

- Continue with this circulating pink energy for as long as it feels good. When you feel ready and energized, open your eyes and clap your hands to bring everything back into focus.

- Close your circle and keep this energy throughout the day. Whenever a negative thought passes through your mind and is ready to come out in the form of a complaint, revert back to your pink light and remember to be the mirror.

MAGICK SUGAR LIP SCRUB

This sugar scrub will help you bring sweetness directly to your lips! Use it intentionally in your makeup routine to receive ALL the kisses.

YOU WILL NEED

1 tbsp granulated sugar • ⅓ tbsp coconut oil • 3 drops of essential rose oil

TIMING

This charm is best performed under New Moon energy to set the seed of sweetness. Libra and Taurus, our romantically Venusian signs, are the best for carrying out this energy.

METHOD

- Ground yourself by focusing on your heart chakra and breathing intentionally into it. Breathe deeply in and out and focus on growing that place of love.

- Mix together the sugar and coconut oil until you have a good scrubbing consistency. As you add the rose oil, envision the sweetness you'd like to receive.

- Using your finger, scoop out a portion of your scrub and rub it on your lips in a counterclockwise motion, keeping your vision in your mind's eye.

- As you rinse off your scrub, shed any doubt that you have about the attention you deserve.

- Close your circle and carry this energy with you throughout the day.

NOTE: Please be mindful of any allergies or sensitivities you may have before carrying out this spell. It's basically impossible to think sweet thoughts with itchy or blistered lips, so try this concoction on a small test patch of skin if you're unsure of how your body will react to it.

CANDY CHARM

It is said that we give out energy through the dominant side of our body and receive energy from the opposite side. So, if you're right-handed, your dominant side, or right side, exerts the energy your body puts into the world. Following suit, your left side would accept energy. This charm will help you to either give or receive sweetness depending on where your charm is placed. Use your energetic sphere and some candy to evoke affection. (You were looking for a reason to go HAM on some drugstore candy, weren't you?)

YOU WILL NEED

A wrapped piece of candy • An outfit with pockets

TIMING

This spell is best performed under a Waxing Moon to bring in the sweetness you desire. Air signs will be great to create an environment of communication and flirtation.

METHOD

- Ground yourself by noticing any tightness in the body, doing a full-body scan starting from the top of your head, down to your toes.

- Take the candy and hold it in your hands. Focus intently on channeling a sweet and sugary energy into your candy, for it will be the vehicle to attract sweetness your way.

- Imagine the candy glowing with a soft pink light, and hold that vision until you feel satisfied.

- Place the candy in your dominant pocket to emit sweetness or in your opposite pocket to receive sweetness.

- Close your circle and carry this magickal candy throughout your day!

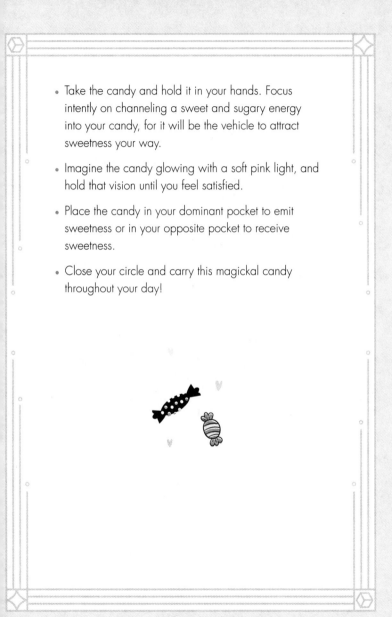

SUGAR BOWL CANDLE SPELL

Candle spells are powerful conduits for setting the mood of a situation as it unfolds over time. Use this one to guide the vibe before a first date or increase a friendly energy between you and the eye of your desire. When you want to be approached with kindness, respect, and adoration, use this spell to sweeten the environment.

YOU WILL NEED

A yellow candle • A dowel • A fire-safe bowl • An abundance of sugar

TIMING

This spell is best performed from a New Moon to a Full Moon to bring in the energy you desire. Air signs will help conversation flow, and Fire signs will warm things up. Leo is most preferable as it is ruled by the Sun and it rules the heart, and will pump up your confidence on your date!

METHOD

- Ground yourself by breathing in positive energy and exhaling harmful thoughts. Sink into the floor beneath you to keep you anchored.

- Hold your candle and start to envision fun and bubbly conversation under the sun. Yellow is connected to the sun and warms up interactions, so use the candle's energy to influence your vision.

- Grab your dowel and carve a name, sigil (see page 64 if you do not have one yet!), or date idea that you want to be the focus of this warm and sweet environment into the candle. Keep this intention in your mind's eye as you carve.

- Place your candle in the bowl and sprinkle it with the sugar. As you sprinkle, repeat, "Keep it light, keep it sweet, this is the energy when we meet," three times.

- Light your candle, focusing your intention into the flame. Close your circle and let the candle burn all the way down. If you can't let it burn safely, snuff it out rather than blowing it out to keep the intention alive, and relight until the candle has finished burning.

SMILE CHARM

This spell might seem a little on the nose, but it works instantly. While lipstick glamour attracts the attention of the outside world, your smile is even more powerful. Whenever you are looking to approach a difficult situation, a smile will immediately set the tone. Try it out in any interaction to witness its power.

YOU WILL NEED

Your smile • A mirror

TIMING

This spell is best performed under New Moon and Waxing Moon energy since you are looking to open up a sweet exchange. Capricorn rules the skeletal system and teeth, so this energy is great for this charm. However, Venusian signs such as Libra and Taurus will add a sensory and romantic aspect to your smile as well.

METHOD

- Ground yourself by breathing in through your teeth and out through pursed lips. Focus directly on your mouth and continue to breathe for as long as it feels right.

- Once you are ready, stare into your mirror and smile! Concentrate on your smile and envision yourself evoking sweetness as you flash your pearly whites.

- Close your circle and carry this energy with you throughout the day.

- Smile before every interaction to use that energy. The magickal charge of your grin will break down anyone's guard and set the tone for a sweet exchange.

KITCHEN WITCHERY SWEETS SPELL

In kitchen witchery, there is a very strong connection between the intentional creation of food and relationships. Whether you are baking from scratch or adding water to a mix from a box, you can powerfully infuse intention by stirring your batter. This spell can be modified for any level of skill. Most important, do what feels good.

YOU WILL NEED

A recipe for any baked good • Your intention!

TIMING

This spell is best performed under New Moon energy to start bringing in the intention. Earth signs are excellent for this spell because they are material and sensory, but Cancer, a true homebody, will also help successfully carry out your desire.

METHOD

- Ground yourself by completing a body scan from the top of your head down to your feet, breathing deeply and intentionally. Once you feel relaxed, get ready to bake!

- Whether you're a master baker or a Betty Crocker devotee, you can still inject your magick into any recipe. Once you begin to stir the batter, it's time to get charming.

- Make sure to stir clockwise, bringing in the energy, and whisper your intention into the batter. As you visualize yourself receiving sweetness from your crush or creating a sweet environment for you and your partner, speak to the batter and let it know exactly what you desire. Continue to follow the recipe instructions to bake and cool your treat before decorating.

- If decorating your treat, consider adding a magickal sigil (see page 64). If you're making something with frosting, you could carve your sigil into your treat and cover it with frosting or draw it on with frosting and then fill in the gaps so no one will see it; only you know it exists. This will help keep a specific intention in mind.

- Close your circle once you have finished creating your baked good.

- Bring your baked goods to your crush or significant other and note your interaction after they've had a taste.

TIP Being mindful of allergies is crucial for this spell. The goal is to provide your crush or loved one with a magickal treat, and an EpiPen will ruin the sweetness.

SINGING WATER BOWL

Water is a very influential conduit, and sound helps to carry your intention into other realms. While you don't have to have pipes like Ariana Grande to perform this effectively, you should perform it in a way that makes you feel confident and certain. If this spell makes you feel a little silly, practice it when you won't be disturbed.

YOU WILL NEED

Filtered water • A bowl • Sugar

TIMING

This spell is best performed in between New Moon energy to Full Moon energy to bring in the intention, but most importantly performed on a Friday, as that is the day of the Goddess. Water signs are best for this type of psychic and ethereal magick to increase emotional connection.

METHOD

- Center yourself by grounding. Do a body scan from the top of your head to your toes, and then focus on your heart chakra, opening yourself up to your desires.

- Pour the water into the bowl, and sprinkle in sugar to add sweetness to the energy.

- Be sure that you are certain of your intention, whether it's starting a sweet chat with your crush, bringing in a new romance, or healing a relationship that has become cold.

- With your hands cupped around your mouth, directed at the bowl, start singing your intention in a trance state. It doesn't have to rhyme, or even make sense. Just sing from your heart and let the water hear you.

- If the thought of this is intimidating, focus on your intention in your head while you hum a soothing tune into the water. You can modify any spell to make you comfortable.

- Close your circle and place your bowl under your bed for seven days, then toss the water outside of your home. Make note of any dreams that may be offering guidance.

CHAPTER 7

PASSION AND DESIRE SPELLS

Ready to heat up the bedroom with some hot goddess fire?

These spells will help create a steamy vibe for you and your boo in the bedroom. Be prepared for more confidence than you've ever had between the sheets. It will lead you to more frequent and intense orgasms. Some of these spells will help invite that energy in, and some will set the scene when it's time to get it on.

Since sex is a sensitive subject, it's important to address consent on behalf of both parties. If you feel uncomfortable or hesitant, don't be afraid to say no and honor how you feel. Confidence and willingness are the main drivers for hot sex, and if either of you are not 100 percent invested in getting it on, the spells will be ill received.

If you have never had sex with the eye of your desire before, perform communication and sweetening spells first to open up the opportunity for a relationship before attempting to manifest a sexual relationship. People deserve a respectful approach, so while your loins may be burnin', focus on taming the beast with a real human connection.

CINNAMON AND TWINE FIRE RITUAL

This spell is excellent for bringing forth a passionate union. With fire-ruled cinnamon as a sort of poppet between you and a potential flame, this spell will help to bring about some real sparks. While the goal of this spell is to focus on the orgasmic energy you want to receive once this spell is in effect, try to keep your mind off of anyone in particular. Use this ritual if you have been through a dry spell and are looking to increase the sex flow to your bedroom.

YOU WILL NEED

Two sticks of cinnamon • Twine •
Cauldron or stove-top pot • Lighter

TIMING

This spell is best performed under New Moon to Full Moon energy so you can welcome a hot climax. Fire signs are perfect for igniting the flame, but Scorpio, the sexiest sign of the zodiac, is ideal for this spell.

METHOD

- Ground yourself by breathing in deeply while you root yourself firmly into the ground. As you imagine being anchored deep into the core of the Earth, visualize a small fire kindling in your belly.

- Take your two sticks of cinnamon and focus that fire energy into them. Imagine having the best orgasm of your life, and send that visualization into your sticks of cinnamon.

- Wrap the twine three times around your cinnamon sticks and then tie them together. During this process repeat the following: "Fire and flame, the best orgasm I will claim."

- As you keep your vision in your mind's eye while repeating your incantation, light the cinnamon and twine with the lighter. It may not burn completely, but once it catches fire, toss it in your cauldron or stovetop pot.

- Wait for the flame to extinguish on its own. Close your circle and toss the cooled ingredients outside of your home.

UP YOUR LIBIDO WITH SEX MAGICK

Sex magick is fabulous for manifestation, but it has another added benefit. The more you explore your body, your senses, and how you react to touch, the more sensitive you will become. You can increase your intuition with sex magick, but you can also train your brain to notice your body's responses, making you a far more sensual lover. If you are self-conscious about your performance in the bedroom, or if you haven't had an orgasm from your partner in ages, this is just the spell for you.

YOU WILL NEED

A comfortable place to explore your desires •
Your fingers

TIMING

This spell is best performed at Full Moon energy. Because it is the climax of light, Full Moons will influence orgasm. Depending on what kind of sexual energy you'd like to provoke, you can choose from Venusian Taurus or Libra for romance, Scorpio for kink and deep desire, or any Fire sign for passion.

METHOD

- Ground yourself by completing a full-body scan and really coming into your skin. Breathe deeply in and out as you move from the top of your head, all the way down to your toes.

- Start to run your fingers over your body lightly, teasing different erogenous zones, like over your neck or down to your thighs. Take some time concentrating on your touch before diving directly into masturbation.

- Rather than using a toy, use your fingers to start exploring your body more strategically, and notice where you start to heat up. There is no right way to do this, and it is definitely not a race to the finish line.

- As you come toward climax, start to imagine a glowing orange light coming from your genitals, opening up your sacral chakra. Keep your vision of the orange light very focused until you reach an orgasm and come back down to relaxation.

- Close your circle and let yourself rest, basking in the afterglow.

CHARM YOUR PANTIES (OFF)

This charm is a strong form of glamour magick that feels like a dirty little secret! If you're going out in search of a one-night stand, this spell is for you. While the magick is fleeting, it's strong in the moment, so if you end up finding a personal connection, ride the wave and see where it goes. However, it's best to perform this spell without any strings attached.

YOU WILL NEED

Your sexiest panties or lingerie

TIMING

This charm is best performed under Full Moon energy to call upon a grand climax. Just be careful of your energetic boundaries at this time because the levels of attraction will be strong AF. Fire signs and Scorpio are the best for wrangling a hot rendezvous.

METHOD

- Ground yourself by breathing in deeply for a count of three and out for a count of three. Repeat this cycle three times.

- Hold your panties in your hands and envision the most confident version of yourself receiving the attention you desire and rocking it in the bedroom. Play this sexy fantasy in your head and infuse those thoughts into your garment.

- As you put on your panties one leg at a time, imagine your sacral chakra glowing bright orange and opening up, inviting in sexual energy.

- Close your circle and carry this energy into the night!

FRUIT ALTAR OFFERING

Items of the Earth carry planetary energies along with masculine and feminine influences. Without getting too deep here, you can determine whether a fruit is masculine or feminine by its shapes! Anything phallic in nature, such as bananas or cucumbers, can be assumed to have masculine energy, while fruits with seeds, like apples, figs, or avocados, would be fertile and feminine. Using this principle, you can offer an intentional fruit to your altar and watch it manifest great sex.

YOU WILL NEED

A love altar • A fruit of your choice • A pen • A sigil

TIMING

This spell is best performed under a New Moon to Waxing Moon to bring in the partner you desire. Earth signs will help to manifest this wish into the material plane.

METHOD

- Ground yourself by sitting in front of your altar, sinking into meditation and connecting to the energy of your sacred space.

- Choose your fruit according to the energy you'd like to attract (masculine or feminine) and use a pen to draw a sigil that represents great sex. If needed, revisit chapter 4 to learn how to create a sigil (page 64).

- Charge your sigil into the fruit of your choice by focusing on the great sex you'll be having.

- Place the fruit on your altar, and thank a Spirit, the Universe, your guides, or whoever makes you most comfortable, for bringing you your dream sex partner.

- Close your circle and remember to toss out your fruit once it begins to rot!

PASSIONATE AROMA SPELL

Certain essential oils are known to heighten the libido. Rose adds a touch of romance, ylang-ylang is a well-known aphrodisiac, and neroli heightens blood flow. This magickal elixir of all three of those ingredients is perfect for creating passion in the bedroom.

YOU WILL NEED

A spray bottle • Filtered water •
Rose essential oil • Ylang-ylang essential oil •
Neroli essential oil

TIMING

This spell is best performed on a Full Moon to bring in the climax you desire. Fire signs or super sultry Scorpio are best for this sort of passion.

METHOD

- Ground yourself by feeling your feet sink into the floor, rooting deeply into the ground.

- Take your spray bottle and fill it with water, imagining that it's glowing bright orange, to represent your sacral chakra. Bonus points if you can find an orange spray bottle!

- Take your essential oils and add a few drops each into the water until you get the desired aroma. Swirl your bottle clockwise to combine the oils and water, imagining you and your partner having the hottest sex you've ever had.

- When you have infused the elixir with your sexy fantasy, take your spray bottle and spray your bedsheets and pillows with a few spritzes on each.

- When you can begin to smell the fragrance to your liking, place the bottle underneath your bed to capture the energy of your sexual romp for an added bonus at its next use.

- Close your circle, and don't worry if the fragrance fades. The essence of the energy is in your sheets and will influence your night accordingly.

VENUS INVOCATION

This spell is similar to the self-love goddess invocation (page 44), but it's more specific and slightly more challenging. Within this invocation, you'll be channeling Venus into your own body in order to have more confidence in your performance. It's kind of like an out-of-body experience, but it will allow you to act how you feel in order to receive the love you deserve. This is best performed on a date where you're ready to go all the way, so feel free to wear the lingerie you've charmed under your clothes while you're out to dinner.

YOU WILL NEED

Sexy lingerie • A mirror

TIMING

This spell is best performed under Full Moon energy, when emotions are running high. Venus signs such as Taurus and Libra are best for this invocation, but Fire signs and Scorpio will also aid in the sexy energy.

METHOD

- Stand naked in front of a mirror. Ground yourself by doing a full-body scan. As you observe the different areas of your body, from the top of your head down to your toes, feel them soften and relax. Try to look at yourself with as much love and affection as you can.

- Take some of your lingerie and hold it in your hands, charging it with intense desire and confidence as you imagine the power of Venus flowing through you.

- Look up into the sky and say with a strong voice, "Venus, I ask you to take hold and guide me through this journey as I entwine my body with another. Help me feel powerful. Flow through me."

- Feel the energy coursing through you as you put on your lingerie. The power of Venus is in you, and you have her guiding you through every motion.

- Close your circle and give your boo the ride of a lifetime.

BEDPOST RITUAL OIL

This spell works best if you have a bed with bedposts, as the title suggests. If not, you can rub the oil on the four corners of your bed frame. Using this oil will create a ritualistic area where you can perform heightened sex magick with the bae. If you're looking to make magick together, this is the spell for you.

YOU WILL NEED

Cinnamon essential oil • Ylang-ylang essential oil

TIMING

This spell is best performed under Full Moon energy. Any sign will help bring your manifestations to life, but if you are looking to achieve something material, shoot for Earth signs.

METHOD

- Ground yourself with your partner by holding hands and doing a body scan from the top of your head down to your feet, breathing deeply and intentionally.

- Take three drops of each essential oil in one of your palms and rub them together until you feel heat.

- Rub the oil clockwise on your bedpost, or in little circles on the frame, starting from the top left corner and continuing in a clockwise motion.

- Envision a glowing orange perimeter connecting your bedposts. Once you have that vision in your mind's eye, you're ready to begin.

- Sex magick essentially works the same with a partner as it does solo, so make sure you are both intentionally moving your bodies and slowly building the passion. If you can reach climax at the same time, your spell will be extra powerful. Be sure that both of you are keeping the goal of your manifestation as you see it in your mind's eye together. Any discrepancies will confuse the Universe.

- Once you are finished, close your circle.

SEXUALITY BATH POTION

Our dreams tell us a lot about what we secretly want. They can be messengers if we open ourselves to receiving them. This bath will help open you up to erotic dreams, which can help you realize what you truly crave in the bedroom. The more we know, the better we can manifest! If you do not have a bathtub, modify by creating this mixture in a bowl in the shower and anointing yourself with it.

YOU WILL NEED

A bath • Anise • Rose petals •
Mugwort • Labradorite or amethyst

TIMING

This spell is best performed under Full Moon energy, when we are most receptive. Water signs are best for this type of psychic and ethereal magick. It is also best to complete this spell at night, before bed.

METHOD

- Center yourself by completing a full-body scan from the top of your head to your toes. While grounding yourself, focus on your Sacral Chakra, opening yourself up to pleasure.

- Run the bath water to your liking and place your ingredients, one by one, into the bath, emptying your mind of any doubt, desire, or thought.

- Place your crystal in the bath, or if you are in the shower, near (but not in) your bowl.

- Enter the bath and breathe deeply. Play with the ingredients by slowly stroking them on your skin. Engage with your senses, and whenever any thought passes through your mind, release it and return to your body.

- When you are done soaking, empty your bath, close your circle.

- Place your crystal under your pillow, and go to sleep.

- When you wake up, note anything significant in your dreams. Dreams speak in symbols, so be open to receiving messages not just as they are, but how they make you feel.

CHAPTER 8

BROKEN HEART AND CORD-CUTTING SPELLS

The most difficult (and almost inevitable) part of love is heartbreak. Some lucky dogs may never experience it, but most of us do, and it hits hard.

These spells are all about tending to your heart, accepting what happened, and releasing the negativity so it will no longer hold you back. When we dwell on past loves, we leave little room to accept a new love in. Sometimes we take up so much subconscious space in our brain that we only manifest what left us hurt. This chapter will help you to reprogram on your own terms.

Use these spells with a lot of tenderness. Rushing to heal is never wise; it takes time. Make sure you don't trigger yourself by going too fast or doing too many spells, and do not drown your feelings in order to "get over it." You deserve as much time as it takes to feel good about releasing the past, and these spells are meant to help you on the journey, not eradicate the pain.

TECH WITCH BANISHMENT

This may seem like common sense to some and nearly impossible to others, but it's a necessary step to start moving on. In the age of technology, residual energy lies at our fingertips 24/7, and we must take measures to establish boundaries that protect our heart. Even the most amicable breakups need time to heal. A constructive and effective way to do this is to get your ex out of sight and out of mind.

YOU WILL NEED

Your phone • Your ex's contact information

TIMING

This spell is best performed under Waning Moon energy. It will help you release. Virgo and Gemini, which are both ruled by Mercury, are best for Tech Witch spells.

METHOD

- Ground yourself by completing a full-body scan from your head down to your toes, sinking into your body. Tech Witch spells are very cerebral so intentionally focus your breath into your whole body for balance.

- Take your phone and, one by one, go into each of your ex's social media accounts, phone numbers, and other possible opportunities of connection.

- Each time you go into an account, go to the "Block" option. Block them while you say, "I release you."

- Remember to breathe deeply through each account.

- Close your circle, and in about two weeks' time, you'll feel renewed. The memory of your ex will turn to dust.

SHADOW WORK RITUAL
FOR PARTNER

If you've already performed the shadow work ritual from chapter 3 (page 42), you know how freeing this type of journaling can be. While it's difficult to bring our shadow into the light, it gives us the power to accept what we can't control and move on. Make sure to firmly ground yourself before you begin your spell and be as honest with yourself as possible. Go slowly if you need to.

YOU WILL NEED

A pen • Paper • Your honesty

TIMING

This spell is best performed under Waning Moon energy so you can release what doesn't serve you. Water signs are excellent for this type of emotional deep dive, but Earth signs will keep you grounded.

METHOD

- Ground yourself by breathing in deeply while you root yourself firmly into the ground. As you imagine being anchored deep into the core of the Earth, become sturdy like a tall tree with flowing branches.

- Take your pen and paper and begin to journal on the following prompts.

    ✦ What do I regret about my previous relationship, and how can I shape it into a lesson?

    ✦ What left me hurt in my previous relationship, and how can I express gratitude for it?

    ✦ What truly served me in the relationship? What didn't? How did I play a part in those roles?

- Meditate on your answers and try to be as nonjudgmental as possible with yourself.

- Close your circle and envision releasing your past into the cosmos.

CLEANSING BATH

TBH, this bath has a strong smell, but it will help to cut the cords between you and your ex. Be sure to not rinse off after the bath, as the purifying and banishing properties of the ingredients must stay on your skin for twenty-four hours to fully dissolve the energy. It's best to perform this spell at home. If you don't have a bathtub, make the mixture in a bowl and anoint yourself with it as you shower.

YOU WILL NEED

Salt • About 1 cup of apple cider vinegar •
Lemons, cut into four rounds • Black pepper

TIMING

This spell is best performed under Dark Moon energy for potent banishing. Water signs are best for bath magick.

METHOD

- Run your bath with lukewarm to cold water and add all of your ingredients.

- Enter the bath and ground yourself by doing a full-body scan from the top of your head down to your toes.

- Take the lemon rounds and start to rub yourself with them in the bath, envisioning the citrus clearing out any resentment, negativity, or hurt.

- Soak in the bath for as long as you want. Just make sure you've covered your whole body, even the soles of your feet, with the lemon rounds. Be cautious of your eyes, and if you are standing in the shower, try not to slip.

- Once you have anointed yourself with the lemon rounds, empty the bath and envision your heartbreak swirling down the drain with the water. If you are in the shower, imagine the water running off of you is taking your pain with it.

- Do not rinse off. Close your circle and head directly to bed. You can shower the next night to rid yourself of the vinegar aroma.

CORD-CUTTING VISUALIZATION

This spell releases emotional ties to your ex-partner. If you still feel a connection, for instance, in your dreams, this spell works wonders. If you have more advanced witch-craft tools like a blade of obsidian, a selenite wand, or an athame, feel free to use them in this spell.

YOU WILL NEED

Obsidian blade (optional) • A selenite wand (optional) • An athame (optional) • Your hand • A broom

TIMING

This ritual is best performed under Waning to Dark Moon energy. Water signs will help you psychically connect to this visualization.

METHOD

- Ground by breathing deeply into your chest, doing a full-body scan from the top of your head to your toes.

- Take whichever tool you have, even if it is the side of your hand in a karate-chop position, and begin to wave it over your body, starting from the top of your head and moving all the way down to the soles of your feet.

- As you wave your tool, imagine actual cords being cut and falling to the ground. All these cords are representative of the ties to your past love.

- Imagine the cords snapping, curling, and twisting to the ground, creating a pile beneath you on the floor.

- Once you have cut every cord, take your broom and visualize yourself sweeping up all of the cords.

- Toss these cords in the toilet and, when you flush, imagine all of the ties going down with the water in the bowl.

- Close your circle and notice any residual energy in your dreams. You may need to repeat this if you still have lingering messages in your dreams.

TIP If you want to make the investment, an athame, or witch's blade, represents the element of Air and is my favorite for this kind of work. Obsidian is a black stone that absorbs negative energy and comes in blade form. A selenite wand is a moon-ruled crystal that has incredible energetic cleansing properties. Otherwise, your hand works just fine.

BLACK SALT BANISHMENT

Black salt is a key ingredient in any Witch's cabinet and is excellent for banishment and protection. Once you make your own, you can use it in a variety of ways to keep you safe, including sprinkling on your doorstep to keep out unwanted visitors. This spell will teach you how to keep your dreams free and clear of any exes so you can sleep without seeing their dumb face.

YOU WILL NEED

Sea salt • Ground black pepper • Charcoal • A mortar and pestle • A sachet

TIMING

This spell is best performed under Waning Moon energy in order to release. Water signs are best when working with dream realms.

METHOD

- Ground yourself by breathing in freedom and exhaling pain. Feel your lungs expanding, and continue breathing deeply until you feel lighter.

- Add your bits of charcoal and ground black pepper to your mortar.

- Grind them together with your pestle until you get a fine black powder.

- Slowly mix in your sea salt, adding pinches until you get a nicely coated black mineral.

- As you mix, imagine yourself having a comfortable night's sleep, free from any dreams or nightmares about your past relationship.

- Place your black salt mixture in your sachet and tie it tight, making sure nothing leaks out, and close your circle.

- Place your sachet under your pillow, and let it work by absorbing your dreams.

CAULDRON YONI BANISHMENT

"Yoni" is the Sanskrit word for "womb" and has been used to describe the vagina or vulva. Although it appears in the title of this spell, you don't need to have a vagina to perform it! It works equally well with all genitalia. The purpose of this spell is to banish the leftover energy from a sexual encounter that you wish to forget, whether it was a flop of a one-night stand or an ex you wish you had never dated.

YOU WILL NEED

Filtered water • A stockpot • Rosemary • Juniper • Basil • A towel

TIMING

This spell is best performed on a Waning Moon to Dark Moon to rid your body of the energy. Fire signs or Air signs are great for this kind of cauldron and steam work.

METHOD

- Ground yourself by completing a full-body scan from the top of your head down to your toes. Stop for a moment at your sacral chakra, located in your lower abdomen, intentionally opening it up.

- Take half a pot of your filtered water and bring it to a boil, and then take it off of the heat.

- Slowly mix in your herbs until you can smell the aroma to your liking.

- Place your pot on the floor, and with your towel around your waist, squat over your pot/cauldron.

- Be very careful to not burn yourself, waiting about five minutes after boiling to see if you can handle the steam. You are dealing with a VERY sensitive area of your body.

- Visualize the energy of that sad sex leaving your body, evaporating with the steam.

- After ten to twenty minutes, the spell has done its work.

- Close your circle and empty your pot in the toilet, flushing away the banishment herbs.

NOTE: This should not be performed if pregnant or if you have an IUD.

FLUSH YOUR PAST

Ah, the toilet. It's a funny vessel, but it's a MUST for a modern Witch! It's the best way get rid of energies that do not serve our best selves. You'll understand this spell as you watch your past disappear down the porcelain throne.

YOU WILL NEED

A pen • Paper • Lighter • Toilet

TIMING

This spell is best performed under Waning Moon energy so you can purge all of your leftover feelings. Fire signs are best for this type of passionate work.

METHOD

- Ground yourself by sinking into the floor in the bathroom, rooting yourself deeply into the Earth.

- Grab your pen and paper and start writing a letter to your ex. Do not hold back and do not censor yourself. This should be free-flowing and passionate. Drop those f-bombs.

- Once you have said everything you wish to say in your letter, use your lighter to light the paper from the bottom up, letting all of the tension go.

- Drop your burning paper into the toilet, and as you flush, repeat, "Animosity won't hold me back, there's nothing keeping me from being on track."

- Close your circle and notice if you feel the release.

FREEZE YOUR EX

This spell should only be used under very specific circumstances and as a last resort, as it gets sticky in terms of free will. This spell is used to stop gossip that an ex is spreading and to stop them from contacting you once the relationship is over if you have already done everything in your power to end it. It's important to mention that this should not be used in lieu of contacting authorities if your safety is at risk.

YOU WILL NEED

A jar • Filtered water • A talisman of your ex, like a photo of them, something they left behind, or their name written on a piece of paper

TIMING

This spell is best performed under Dark Moon energy, when banishment is most potent. Scorpio and Aries, warriors ruled by Mars, are best for this kind of work.

METHOD

- Ground yourself by breathing in for a count of three and exhaling for a count of three. When you breathe in, notice your lungs filling up with power, then exhale with gusto.

- Take your jar and fill it about three-quarters of the way with your filtered water.

- Then take the talisman of your ex and place it in the jar. Imagine that they are moving on with their lives, forgetting you existed, and stopping in their tracks when they begin to move toward you. Create a barrier around you and your life in your mind's eye.

- Place your jar in the back of your freezer and forget about it. If you remove the frozen jar prematurely, your ex's attention may return to you. Hide it behind the frozen peas you'll never eat and let it fade from your memory.

- Once you are finished, close your circle, and breathe a sigh of relief.

CHAPTER 9

FINAL THOUGHTS

If there is one thing that is for certain in this world, it is that you are worthy of pure and true love.

If there is a second thing for certain, it is that pure and true love will look different over time. Allow your perspective on sex and relationships to shift and grow as you do, and learn to let go of things that don't serve you anymore.

Self-love and boundaries are the most crucial ingredient of any successful partnership. An empowered Witch is the best foundation for strong, lasting love.

As you continue to flip through this book for reference over the course of your enchanted love life, remember that you are magical AF and deserve for all of your dreams to come true.

If you ever have issues remembering that, use these affirmations:

AFFIRMATIONS

- I am worthy of pure and true love.

- I am not broken; I never needed fixing. I am whole on my own.

- I am beautiful, strong, and powerful.

- I deserve a partner who will uplift and support me.

- I bring so much to the table.

- I have the energy of the Goddess coursing through my veins.

- I attract relationships that are worthy of my time, energy, and value.

- I attract healthy people that support my dreams.

- I attract hot, heavy, and passionate sex.

- I am enough.

HEARST
books

HEARST BOOKS and COSMOPOLITAN are registered trademarks and
the distinctive Hearst Books logo and Cosmopolitan logos are trademarks
of Hearst Magazine Media, Inc.

© 2019 Hearst Magazine Media, Inc.

ISBN 978-1-61837-308-3

Hearst Magazine Media, Inc. has made every effort to ensure that all
information in this publication is accurate. However, due to differing conditions, tools,
and individual skills, Hearst Magazine Media, Inc. cannot be responsible for any
injuries, losses, and/or damages that may result from the use of
any information in this publication.

Distributed in Canada by Sterling Publishing Co., Inc.
c/o Canadian Manda Group, 664 Annette Street
Toronto, Ontario M6S 2C8, Canada
Distributed in Australia by NewSouth Books
University of New South Wales, Sydney, NSW 2052, Australia

For information about custom editions, special sales, and premium
and corporate purchases, please contact Sterling Special Sales
at 800-805-5489 or specialsales@sterlingpublishing.com.

Manufactured in Canada

2 4 6 8 10 9 7 5 3 1

sterlingpublishing.com
cosmopolitan.com

Cover design by Elizabeth Mihaltse Lindy
Interior design by Nancy Singer

Image credits: DEPOSITPHOTOS.COM: @ourlifelooklikeballoon.hotmail.com 46, 53,
101 (mirrors); VECTEEZY.COM 57 (scissors); 83, 127 (phone); 115 (banana);
NANCY SINGER: 65; FREEPIK: 37; 46 (lipstick); 50 (heart); 53 (mascara); 61 (cauldron);
70 (speech bubble); 95 (jar); 97; 101 (lips); 124, 127 (heart) MACROVECTOR 59;
88 (honey jar) NATKACHEVA 45; 46 (lips); 113 RAWPIXEL.COM 88, 95, 123 (flowers);
SHUTTERSTOCK: ISAEKA11 57 (magazines); LENA NIKOLAEVA 2; 4; 20; 30; 33; 34;
49 (hand); 50 (arrow); 61 (branch); 69; 70 (hearts, icons); 75; 79; 88 (flowers, hearts,
butterfly); 95 (bottle);106; 115 (pear, cherries);123 (crystal); 124 (arrows, ornaments); 141;
TANOR 49 (girl); YEROMA (border design throughout)